Current Events and You

An Analysis of How News Affects Your Personal Life

BABY PROFESSOR
EDUCATION KIDS

First Edition, 2020

Published in the United States by Speedy Publishing LLC, 40 E Main Street, Newark, Delaware 19711 USA.

© 2020 Baby Professor Books, an imprint of Speedy Publishing LLC

Baby Professor Books are available at special discounts when purchased in bulk for industrial and sales-promotional use. For details contact our Special Sales Team at Speedy Publishing LLC, 40 E Main Street, Newark, Delaware 19711 USA. Telephone (888) 248-4521 Fax: (210) 519-4043.

10 9 8 7 6 * 5 4 3 2 1

Print Edition: 9781541977785
Digital Edition: 9781541977921

See the world in pictures. Build your knowledge in style.
www.speedypublishing.com

Table Of Contents

H ave you ever heard of the *Pony Express?* You no doubt know that a pony is a baby horse and you most likely know that one meaning of the word express is something that happens or moves at a fast speed. Together, Pony Express refers to a mail delivery system that was used for roughly an eighteen-month period in the early 1860s. Mail was delivered by a person riding a horse. Because the delivery happened from Missouri to California, it was considered a connection to the West.

PONY EXPRESS STATUE IN
OLD SACRAMENTO HISTORIC
DISTRICT, CALIFORNIA

CURRENT EVENTS ARE THINGS OR EVENTS THAT ARE HAPPENING AT THE PRESENT TIME.

In the United States today, people do not have to rely on slow methods to send or receive information. Information is readily available at high speeds. People learn about current events all the time. *Current* refers to right now, or at the present time. Thus, current events are things or events that are happening at the present time. They are reported in the news.

The news is available through many forms of media; some examples of media include the radio, newspapers, television, magazines and the Internet. You can find out about current events by researching them at the library or any of type of media.

Newspaper

TV

Internet

Magazine

Radio

Billboard

THE NEWS IS AVAILABLE THROUGH MANY FORMS OF MEDIA.

CURRENT EVENTS CAN HAVE AN IMPACT ON YOUR PERSONAL LIFE.
NEW TECHN
NEWS

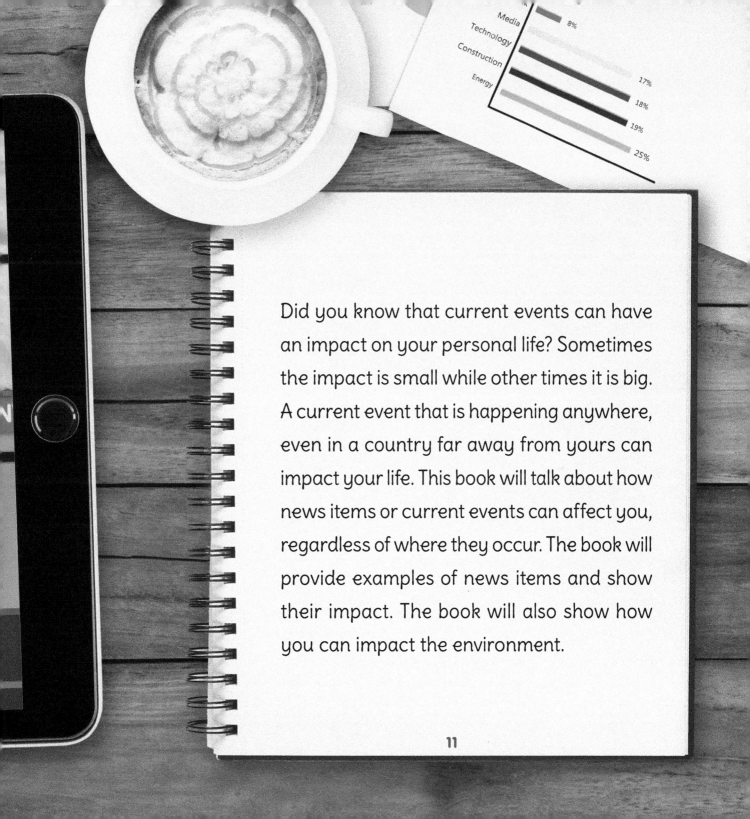

Media 8%

Technology

Construction

Energy

17%

18%

19%

25%

Did you know that current events can have an impact on your personal life? Sometimes the impact is small while other times it is big. A current event that is happening anywhere, even in a country far away from yours can impact your life. This book will talk about how news items or current events can affect you, regardless of where they occur. The book will provide examples of news items and show their impact. The book will also show how you can impact the environment.

Weather Reports and How They Affect Us

O ne common topic reported in the news is the weather. Weather reports describe the weather conditions locally, in one's own area, nationally, in one's own country and internationally, in other countries.

Weather News

WEATHER REPORTS DESCRIBE THE WEATHER CONDITIONS LOCALLY, NATIONALLY AND INTERNATIONALLY.

WEATHER CONDITION

MON
25°C

24°C   26°C   23°C   24°C

25°C

JAN   FEB   MAR   APR   MAY

5304   1756   1923   284

PEOPLE CHECK THE WEATHER FIRST
THING IN THE MORNING.

Media

Technology

Construction

Energy

8%

17%

18%

19%

25%

Weather can be defined as the conditions in the air or the atmosphere at a specific time. It has many different effects. There are many weather conditions, some of which include, rain, snow, dryness, cloudiness, sunshine, wind force and temperature. When people get up in the morning, they often check the weather conditions.

People make many decisions based on what is happening weather wise. Some decisions are made because of the weather conditions in one's local area. For example, if it is hot and sunny, people may opt to wear loose or thin clothes to keep themselves as cool as possible. People may wear a hat or some other form of head covering to protect themselves from being exposed to the sun for a long time.

A GIRL WEARING LOOSE CLOTHES AND HAT TO KEEP HERSELF AS COOL AS POSSIBLE IN HOT AND SUNNY WEATHER.

A WOMAN SAD AND UNHAPPY AT THE AIRPORT WITH FLIGHT CANCELED.

Media 8%

Technology

Construction

Energy 17%

18%

19%

25%

Other decisions are made based on weather conditions elsewhere. For example, if you were going to fly to a place that was experiencing a severe thunderstorm or dense fog, your flight may be cancelled. Although the weather may be fine in your local area, the weather in another place affects you.

Different weather conditions affect the food supply. For example, a drought, which is a long period when no rainfall occurs, has a very damaging effect. The ground is too dry to produce good crops or any crops at all.

A SAD FARMER IS SITTING IN AN AGRICULTURAL FIELD DURING THE LONG DROUGHT.

Another example of how the weather affects the food supply is through too much rain. When there is too much rain, the soil can become washed away. Crops cannot thrive if the soil is not suitable to sustain them.

EXCESSIVE RAINS HAVE SWOLLEN IRRIGATION DITCHES THAT NOW FLOOD THE AGRICULTURAL LAND.

Not only are the people who live where the weather conditions are disrupting the food supply negatively affected, people in other areas are too. Not every place contains farmland. In today's world, food is transported to both near and faraway places. For example, a lot of produce, different fruits and vegetables, are grown in the state of California. They are shipped to many places, both in the United States and other countries. Even if you do not live in California, a drought that hits California, can have an impact on your personal life.

FOOD IS TRANSPORTED TO BOTH NEAR AND FARAWAY PLACES.

Perhaps your favorite fruit is strawberries and you buy strawberries that are grown in California. Because strawberries rely on a good wet growing season, they will either not be grown, or special conditions will have to be made to grow them. If the former happens, you will not be able to have your favorite fruit. If the latter is possible, you still may not be able to have your favorite fruit but even if you do, you will have to pay a hefty price.

KID HOLDING STRAWBERRIES IN A SUPERMARKET.

When there is not enough food, the price of the food increases. Thus, weather conditions can affect what you can eat and the price you pay for it!

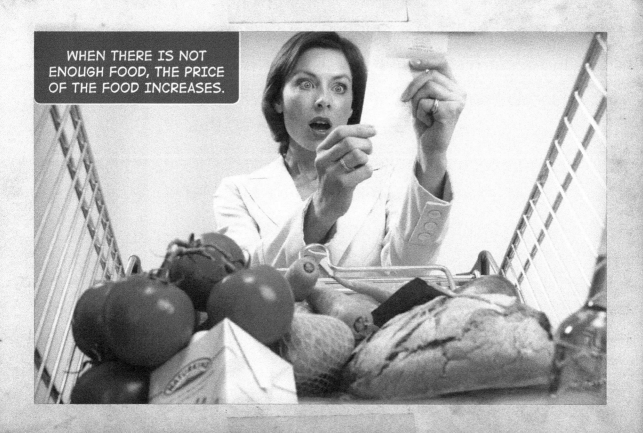

WHEN THERE IS NOT ENOUGH FOOD, THE PRICE OF THE FOOD INCREASES.

Sometimes weather events that are reported in the news motivate people to help others. One example of a devastating weather event in recent history was Hurricane Andrew. Florida was hard hit by the hurricane and there was a lot of damage. However, the damage could have been much more severe if LANDSAT satellites were not able to supply information on the whereabouts of the hurricane. This is a way in which technology can help with getting news of weather conditions to people.

TIME EXPOSURE SATELLITE IMAGE SHOWING HURRICANE ANDREW PASSING OVER FLORIDA, USA, (CENTRE) INTO THE GULF OF MEXICO (LOWER LEFT).

AN AERIAL VIEW OF SOME DAMAGE CAUSED BY HURRICANE ANDREW.

Media

Technology

Construction

Energy

8%

17%

18%

19%

25%

Because the media was able to report the effects of the hurricane, people from other places traveled to Florida to assist in cleaning up the damage. A lot of other people sent along goods to help. Even before the arrival of Hurricane Andrew, advanced technology made it possible for people to prepare.

Long Lasting Effects of Weather Patterns Reported in the News

One example of a weather pattern that has been affecting the Earth for quite a few years is El Niño. This weather pattern has been given a lot of media attention and its effects are widespread. El Niño happens as a result of a temperature increase in the area of the Pacific Ocean off the shores of Peru. Although Peru is in South America, the weather pattern can impact weather conditions worldwide. Once the water reaches a certain temperature, it causes the air temperature to also increase. This in turn, results in climatic changes all over our planet.

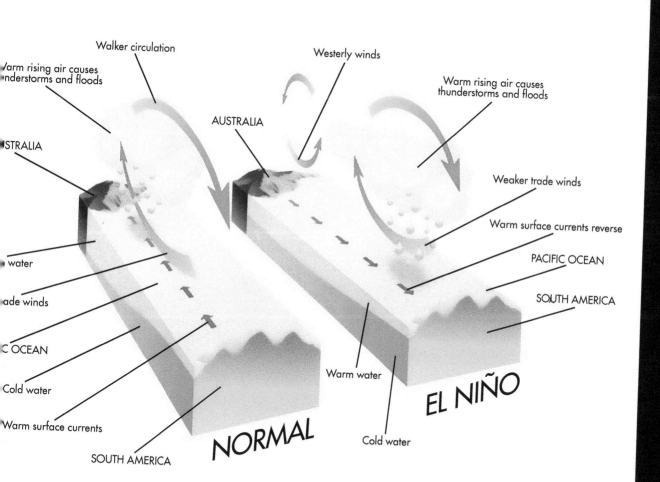

Walker circulation

Westerly winds

Warm rising air causes thunderstorms and floods

Warm rising air causes thunderstorms and floods

AUSTRALIA

Weaker trade winds

STRALIA

Warm surface currents reverse

water

PACIFIC OCEAN

ade winds

SOUTH AMERICA

C OCEAN

Cold water

Warm water

Warm surface currents

Cold water

NORMAL

EL NIÑO

SOUTH AMERICA

SCIENTIFIC ILLUSTRATION OF THE CAUSES AND EFFECTS OF EL NINO.

El Niño is something that occurs on a regular basis. In the latter part of the 1990s, when it resulted in the water temperature to be the highest ever recorded in history, some parts of the Earth experienced awful weather conditions.

Although scientists are not exactly sure the reasons for El Niño, some of them think that it may have a connection to another weather phenomenon called global warming. This weather phenomenon is when the temperature of our planet starts to rise.

CORAL BLEACHING CAUSED BY EL NINO, A CONSEQUENCE OF GLOBAL WARMING, MALDIVES.

GLOBAL WARMING MAY HAVE SERIOUS REPERCUSSIONS,
UNFAVORABLE CONSEQUENCES FOR THE ENTIRE EARTH.

Media

Technology

Construction

Energy

8%

17%

18%

19%

25%

Some scientists think that global warming, in turn, may have serious repercussions, unfavorable consequences, for the entire Earth. It is thought that with global warming, changes in weather patterns will occur. Related to this problem is that some scientists fear that the temperature of the Earth is increasing at a dangerous pace. If the Earth's temperature increases too fast, then serious issues could be the result and these issues would reach many places in the world.

Air pollution is a contributing factor to global warming. Air pollution happens when things that are harmful or toxic are released into the air. Air pollution comes from many sources, most of which can be stopped or restricted.

FACTORIES RELEASE SULFUR DIOXIDE INTO THE AIR.

MOTOR VEHICLES RELEASE HARMFUL CARBON MONOXIDE.

Media
Technology
Construction
Energy

8%

17%

18%

19%

25%

One source of air pollution is the carbon monoxide that comes from using motor vehicles. Another source is sulfur dioxide that is released into the air from certain factories.

Another source is the burning of fossil fuels. Fossil fuels are the remains of dead plants and animals that lived on the Earth millions of years ago. Some examples of fossils fuels are coal, natural gas or oil.

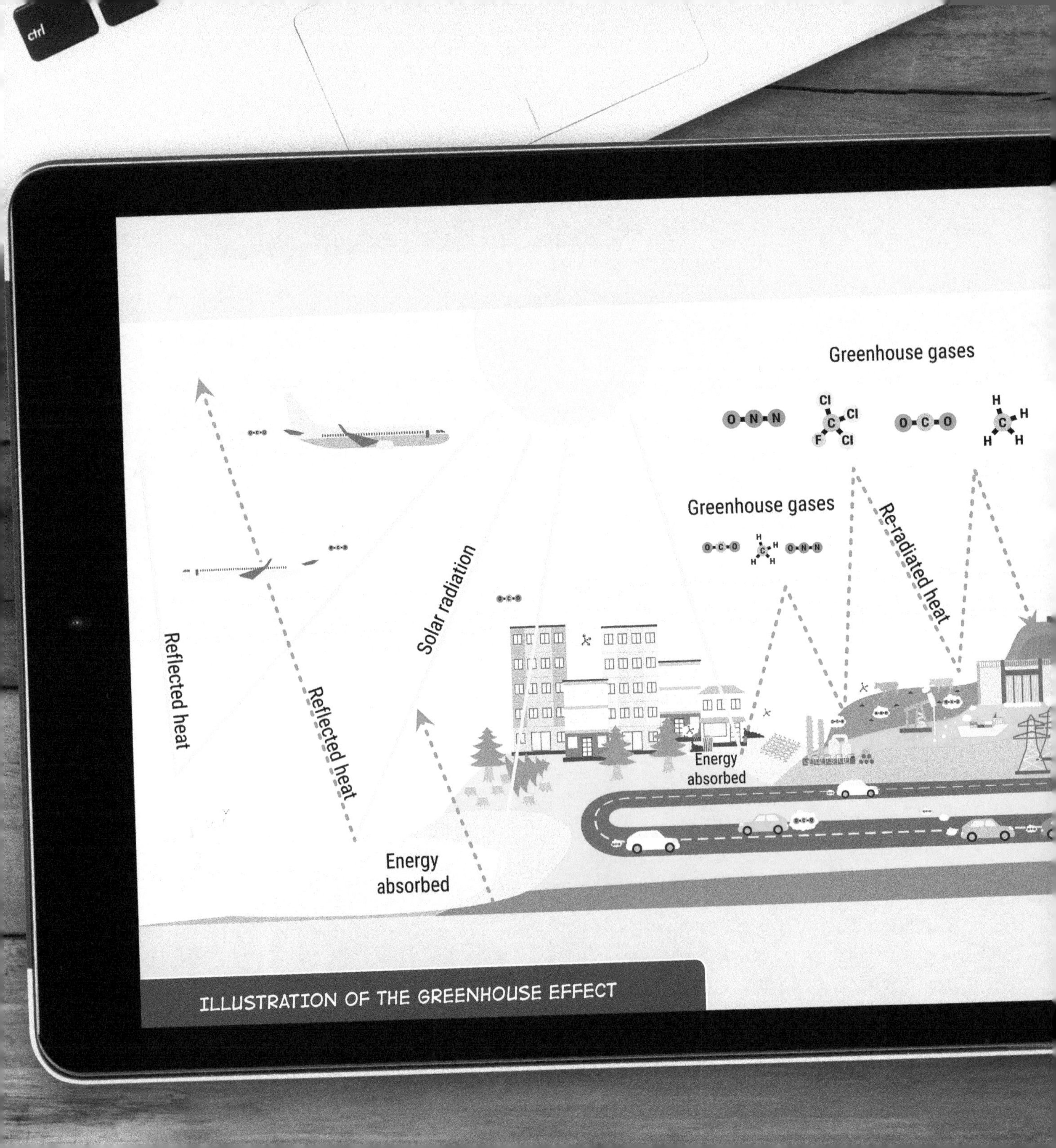

Greenhouse gases

Greenhouse gases

Re-radiated heat

Reflected heat

Reflected heat

Solar radiation

Energy absorbed

Energy absorbed

ILLUSTRATION OF THE GREENHOUSE EFFECT

When garbage or fossil fuels are burned, they emit, or let off, gases. These gases rise and go into the Earth's atmosphere. Some scientists think that once they are there, they prevent heat from escaping the Earth's atmosphere. Because the heat from air pollution remains inside the atmosphere, the temperature of the Earth has increased. The term used to describe this condition is the greenhouse effect.

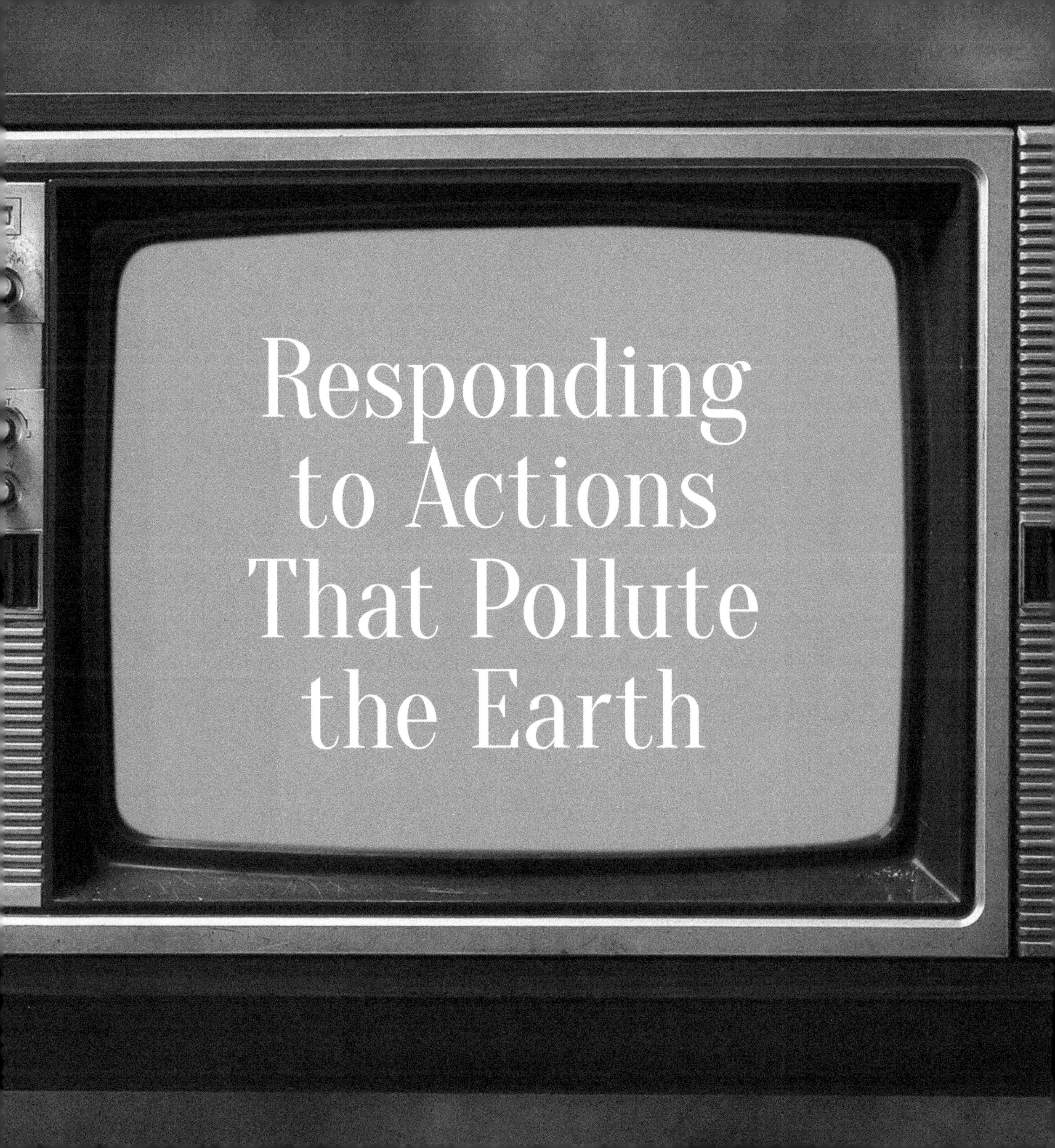

Responding to Actions That Pollute the Earth

There are ways in which pollution can be reduced. Some actions would require the intervention of governments and businesses. Other actions can be taken by ordinary citizens everywhere. You can help by reducing or reusing the number of items you use. For example, instead of always buying a new bottle of water, you can put your water in a reusable cup.

COTTON NET BAG WITH METAL WATER BOTTLE, BAMBOO CUTLERY, BAMBOO LUNCH BOX AND REUSABLE COFFEE CUP.

RECYLING IS ONE OF THE WAYS TO TACKLE THE PROBLEM OF POLLUTION.

Another way in which the problem of pollution can be tackled is through recycling. This is a process in which used items are transformed or made into different items instead of being discarded into the garbage.

Once an item has been tossed into the garbage, it does not disappear. It may get burned or it may be put into a landfill. Neither of these methods of garbage disposal are good for our planet. They help contribute to pollution in the air, the ground and the oceans.

GARBAGE TRUCK DUMPING GARBAGE ON A LANDFILL

TREES ARE ONE OF EARTH'S NATURAL RESOURCES.

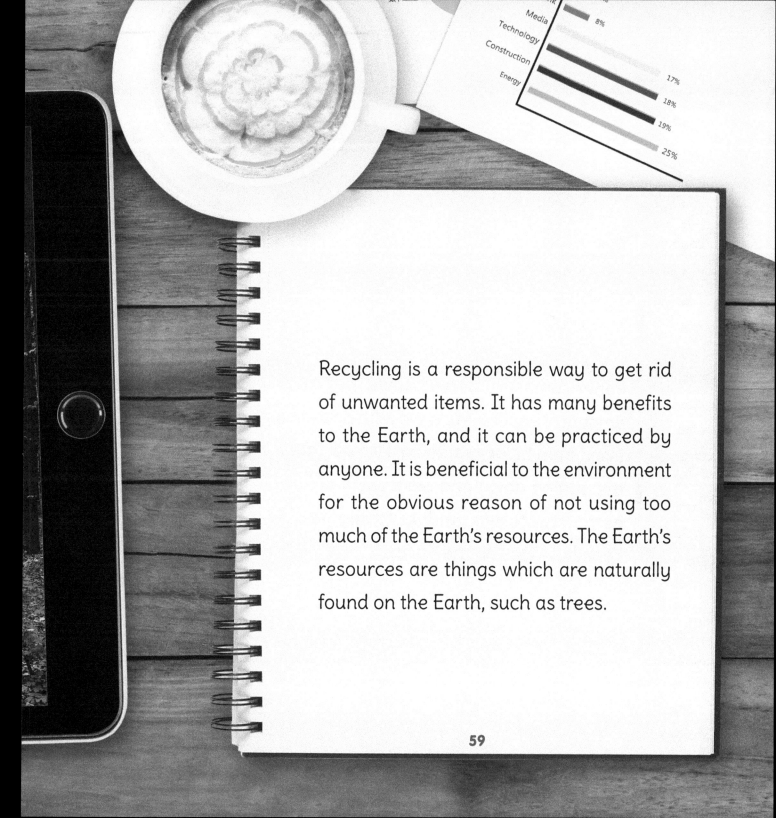

Recycling is a responsible way to get rid of unwanted items. It has many benefits to the Earth, and it can be practiced by anyone. It is beneficial to the environment for the obvious reason of not using too much of the Earth's resources. The Earth's resources are things which are naturally found on the Earth, such as trees.

Paper comes from trees. If we reduce the amount of paper we use, we will help to keep trees from being cut down. Deforestation, the cutting down and destroying of large areas of forested land, is having terrible consequences on the Earth.

DEFORESTATION OF THE MOUNTAIN IN CANAKKALE, TURKEY.

PAPER WASTE AND GARBAGE SUITABLE FOR RECYCLING

There are many paper products and they are used by people all over the world. You may not realize all the paper products that one household can use. Some examples are cardboard boxes, newspapers, coloring books, junk mail, and paper for the printer. Instead of tossing these paper products in the garbage, it is much better to recycle them.

Once paper products have dirt or other unwanted materials removed from them, they are put into piles and brought to a paper mill. Here, they go through a process which makes them able to be used to make new paper products.

PAPER RECYCLING AND PRODUCTION IN A PAPER MILL WITH MACHINE FOR SORTING AND WASHING WASTE PAPER

PLASTIC, GLASS, METAL AND PAPER GARBAGE FOR RECYCLING.

In addition to paper products being recycled, other materials such as glass, plastic and metals can be recycled. Just as with paper, glass, plastic and metal items are cleaned and sent to factories where they are put through a process. At the end of the process, new material is available, and it can be used to make new products.

Media

Technology

Construction

Energy

8%

17%

18%

19%

25%

In today's world, current events are reported through various forms of media. Events can affect us on a personal level despite where they happen. Some events occur locally, as in a basketball tournament in your neighborhood arena. Other events are global, such as an environmental problem that affects every place on Earth.

CURRENT EVENTS ARE REPORTED THROUGH VARIOUS FORMS OF MEDIA.

Some effects of current events are very damaging to the Earth. We can do our part to help by recycling a lot of our garbage. For more information about how to discover current events and do research on them, look for more Baby Professor books on this topic.

Visit

www.speedypublishing.com

To view and download free content on your favorite subject and browse our catalog of new and exciting books for readers of all ages.